CIVIL WAR CHRONICLES

EXTRAORDINARY PEOPLE

By Ruth Ashby

For Ernie   —R.A.

Published by Smart Apple Media
1980 Lookout Drive, North Mankato, Minnesota 56003

Produced by Byron Preiss Visual Publications, Inc.

Library of Congress Cataloging-in-Publication Data
Ashby, Ruth.
Extraordinary people / by Ruth Ashby
v. cm. — (Civil War chronicles)
Contents: Oliver Wendell Holmes, Jr. — Sam Watkins — Joshua Lawrence
Chamberlain — "Stonewall" Jackson — Sergeant William H. Carney — Rose
O'Neal Greenhow — Dorothea Dix — Robert Smalls — Mathew Brady —
Charlotte Forten — Walt Whitman.
ISBN 1-58340-182-2
1. United States—History—Civil War, 1861-1865—Biography—Juvenile literature.
[1. United States—History—Civil War, 1861-1865—Biography.] I. Title.

E467 .A74 2002
973.7'092'2—dc21   2002017644
[B]

First Edition
9 8 7 6 5 4 3 2 1

Contents

Introduction

The Civil War was the great American tragedy. From 1861 to 1865, it divided states, broke up families, took the lives of more than half a million people, and left much of the country in ruins. But it also abolished the great national shame of slavery and cleared the way for the astounding expansion of American industry and culture in the second half of the 19th century. Without the war, the United States would not have been so progressive or so united—and millions of its people would still have been in chains. In the end it was, perhaps, a necessary tragedy.

The conflict had loomed for decades. From the Constitutional Convention in 1787 on, the North and South had disagreed about whether slavery should exist in the United States. In the North, slavery was gradually abolished between 1780 and 1827. But the South became ever more yoked to slavery as its economy became more dependent on the production of cotton. In the meantime, the United States was expanding westward. Every time a territory became a new state, the government had to decide whether it would be slave or free. For 40 years, Congress reached compromise after compromise.

Finally, differences could no longer be bandaged over. With the election of Republican Abraham Lincoln to the presidency in 1860, a crisis was reached. Southern states were afraid that Lincoln, who opposed slavery in the territories, would try to abolish it in the South as well—and that their economy and way of life would be destroyed. On December 20, 1860, South Carolina seceded from the Union. It was

⊠ Abraham Lincoln

⊠ Jefferson Davis

Robert E. Lee ⊠

Ulysses S. Grant ⊠

followed by Alabama, Florida, Georgia, Louisiana, Mississippi, Texas, Virginia, North Carolina, Tennessee, and Arkansas.

The rebellious states formed a new nation, the Confederate States of America, and elected a president, Jefferson Davis. On April 12, 1861, Confederate forces fired on the Federal post of Fort Sumter in Charleston Harbor—and the Civil War began. It lasted four years and touched the lives of every man, woman, and child in the nation. There were heroes on both sides, in the army and on the home front, from Union general Ulysses S. Grant and Confederate general Robert E. Lee to black leader Harriet Tubman and poet and nurse Walt Whitman. It is estimated that at least 620,000 soldiers were killed, almost as many Americans as in all other armed conflicts combined. When Lincoln issued the Emancipation Proclamation on January 1, 1863, and freed the slaves in the rebellious states, it became not just a war for reunification but a war of liberation as well.

Extraordinary People tells the memorable story of some of the thousands of people who made a special contribution of body and spirit during the Civil War.

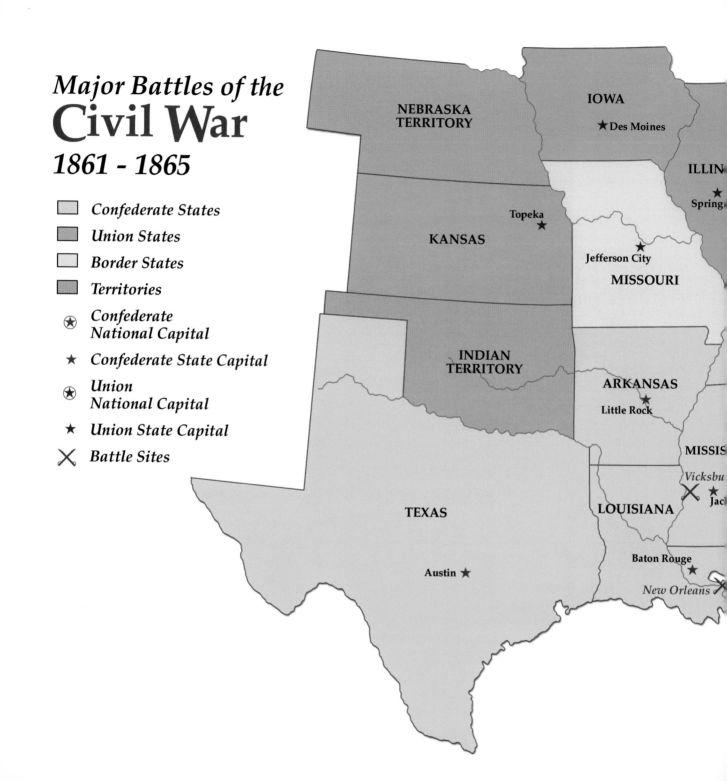

Major Battles of the
Civil War
1861 - 1865

- Confederate States
- Union States
- Border States
- Territories
- ⊛ Confederate National Capital
- ★ Confederate State Capital
- ⊛ Union National Capital
- ★ Union State Capital
- ✕ Battle Sites

NEBRASKA TERRITORY

IOWA
★ Des Moines

ILLIN

Spring

KANSAS

Topeka ★

Jefferson City ★

MISSOURI

INDIAN TERRITORY

ARKANSAS
★
Little Rock

MISSIS

Vicksbu ✕ ★ Jac

TEXAS

LOUISIANA

Baton Rouge
★

Austin ★

New Orleans ✕

BATTLES (on map below)

1 *Gettysburg*
2 *Antietam*
3 *Shenandoah Campaign*
4 *First and Second Manassas*
5 *Wilderness*
6 *Fredericksburg*
7 *Spotsylvania*
8 *Chancellorsville*
9 *Cold Harbor*
10 *Seven Days' Battles*
11 *Petersburg*
12 *Peninsular Campaign*
13 *First and Second Hampton Roads*

Chapter One

Extraordinary People

War is for the participants a test of character; it makes bad men [and women!] worse and good men better.

—*Joshua Lawrence Chamberlain*

In the end, the Civil War was a total war. Nearly everyone in the United States, North and South, found his or her life touched or transformed by the seemingly endless struggle. For soldiers on both sides, it offered the supreme challenge, calling up reserves of stamina and courage many did not know they possessed. Death and despair were all around, failure imminent, glory fleeting or nonexistent. Yet many found comfort in the comradeship of fellow soldiers and the common pursuit of a vital goal. Yankees were fighting for the preservation of the Union, rebels for honor of the Confederacy; both could justly feel that they were fighting for a cause greater than themselves.

Civilians, too, suffered hardship and personal loss. Roused by the excitation of war, many seized the opportunity to make a difference outside the spheres of their ordinary lives. They taught, they nursed, and they spied; they manufactured armaments, harvested crops, took photographs, and wrote poetry. They did what they could.

This book presents some of the Civil War participants whose lives, "touched by fire," would never be the same again.

A Confederate soldier killed at the Battle of Gettysburg. ⊠

Chapter Two

Military Heroes

Joshua Lawrence Chamberlain (1828–1914)

Knight of the Union Army

It was April 12, three days after General Robert E. Lee surrendered to Ulysses S. Grant at Appomattox. Brigadier General Joshua L. Chamberlain, who had been chosen to receive the formal surrender of the Confederate troops, was waiting for the arrival of Confederate General John B. Gordon and his brigade. As Gordon approached, with "heavy spirit and downcast face," Chamberlain ordered his men to "carry arms" as a salute of honor. Chamberlain remembered many years later that Gordon immediately dropped "the point of his sword to his boot toe; then facing to his own command, [gave] word for his successive brigades to pass us with the same position of the manual—honor answering honor." One by one, the Confederate brigades approached to stack their arms and lay down their colors (regimental flags). For the consideration shown to his defeated troops that day, Gordon later called Chamberlain "one of the knightliest soldiers."

Chamberlain was known for his high ideals and gentlemanly conduct. A language professor from Bowdoin College, Maine, he had entered military service at age 34 despite the objections of his family and his colleagues. Because he was an educated man, he was

⊠ Joshua Lawrence Chamberlain, the hero of Little Round Top. Intelligent, courageous, and resourceful, he has been described as "one of the most remarkable officers in the history of the United States."

Quick Facts

★ An estimated 1.5 to 2.2 million men served in the Union forces during the Civil War. An estimated 900,000 served in the Confederate army.

★ An estimated 620,000 soldiers died during the war. Of these, 400,000—65 percent—died of disease.

★ The largest age group of soldiers who served in the Civil War—40 percent—were 21 years old or younger.

★ Eighteen percent of Confederate generals and 8 percent of Union generals died from battle wounds.

★ Approximately 1,200 soldiers received the Medal of Honor in the Civil War. Of these, 17 were black.

★ A total of 166 black regiments, made up of nearly 180,000 troops, served in the U.S. Army, and nearly 20,000 black sailors saw duty in the U.S. Navy.

★ White privates in the Union army generally received $13 per month. Black privates received $10. From this $10, $3 was automatically deducted for clothing. White soldiers, on the other hand, did not lose a clothing allowance. In June 1864, Congress retroactively granted equal pay to black soldiers.

★ Major Martin R. Delany was the first black field officer in the U.S. Army.

★ The Civil War minié ball, made of soft lead, had a hollow base that expanded when fired. Its distinctive spin made the ball deadly accurate.

★ When General Robert E. Lee heard that Stonewall Jackson's arm had been amputated, he said, "Tell him to make haste and get well, and come back to me as soon as he can. He has lost his left arm, but I have lost my right arm."

Chamberlain in dress uniform. ⚔

appointed lieutenant colonel of the 20th Regiment of Maine Volunteers. The 20th Maine fought in numerous engagements, including Fredericksburg in December 1862. After the battle, Chamberlain was trapped on the frozen field for the night. There, listening to the cries of the wounded, he learned the true cost of war. Years later, he still recalled that "some [of the wounded were] breathing inarticulate agony; some dear home names; some begging for a drop of water, some for a caring word; some praying God for strength to bear; some for life; some quick death. We did what we could, but how little that was. . . . "

The encounter that would secure Chamberlain's reputation came at Gettysburg on July 2, 1863. The commander of his brigade, Colonel Strong Vincent, ordered Chamberlain and the 20th Maine to hold the extreme left flank of the mile-long (1.6 km) Union line at a hill called Little Round Top. As the 15th Alabama charged and charged again, the Maine boys held firm until, as one solider remembered, "the blood stood in puddles in some places on the rocks." Then, nearly out of ammunition, Chamberlain decided to seize the initiative. "I stepped to the colors," he recalled. "The men turned towards me. One word was enough—'BAYONET!' It caught like fire and swept along the ranks. They took it up with one shout" and charged down the hill. Caught by surprise, the rebels retreated. Little Round Top remained in Union hands.

✠ Soldiers lie dead at Little Round Top, Gettysburg.

Chamberlain participated in more than 20 engagements in the Civil War, was wounded six times, and had six horses shot out from under him. He became known as a kind and attentive commander to his men, making sure that the sick and wounded had the best of care. One of the soldiers he attended on the battlefield told him that he had "the soul of a lion and the heart of a woman." At Petersburg in June 1864, Chamberlain himself almost died when a minié ball, a rifle bullet with a conical head, passed through both his hips. The wound was so severe that Grant promoted Chamberlain to brigadier general on the spot. (Soldiers were not usually promoted on the battlefield itself.) But thanks to some extraordinarily skillful surgery, he pulled through.

Chamberlain lived to receive the Congressional Medal for Honor in 1893 for his actions at Gettysburg. After the war he served as president of Bowdoin College and governor of Maine for four years. When Joshua Lawrence Chamberlain died at age 86, it was of the old war wound he had received so long ago at Petersburg.

Thomas J. "Stonewall" Jackson (1824–1863)

Stalwart Confederate General

(below): General Thomas J. ✉ "Stonewall" Jackson, the irreplaceable Confederate commander.

(below, right): Jackson's Mill ✉ near Weston, Virginia (now West Virginia), where Jackson lived with his uncle after his parents died.

Thomas J. "Stonewall" Jackson was a peculiar man. Convinced that one of his arms was heavier than the other, he often held it straight up in the air to let the blood flow back into his body. He sat perfectly straight to keep his internal organs aligned, and sucked lemons constantly to aid his digestion. Strict and devout, he didn't swear, drink, or gamble. He used to go into battle with his arms upraised in prayer. But when he got there, he performed brilliantly.

Born in western Virginia, Jackson was raised by an uncle after his parents died. There didn't seem to be much of a future for the orphaned boy until he won an appointment to the United States Military Academy at West Point at age 18. Jackson served with distinction in the Mexican War (1846–1848) and later taught, badly, at the Virginia Military Academy. His students thought he was dull and tried to have him removed.

When the Civil War broke out, Jackson left with some cadets to join the Confederate army. Jackson was placed in charge of a brigade and

soon promoted to brigadier general. It was during the First Battle of Bull Run on July 21, 1861, that the Jackson legend began. At one point in the battle, it looked as if the Union might win. Confederate troops started retreating—but not Jackson. Calm and steady, he kept his brigade in line. "Look at Jackson standing like a stone wall!" another general called out to encourage his men. The rebel troops rallied, the Confederates won the day, and Jackson earned his legendary nickname, "Stonewall."

Jackson's next triumph came in the Shenandoah Valley Campaign in spring 1862. The Shenandoah Valley runs 150 miles (241 km) north through Virginia toward Washington, D.C., and Confederate troops there directly threatened the Union capital. Jackson's mission was to tie up Federal troops in the valley so that they couldn't join the main Union army in southern Virginia. Up and down the valley he marched his men, sometimes more than 35 miles (56 km) a day. They moved so quickly that they started calling themselves "Jackson's Foot Cavalry." The frustrated Union command didn't know where Jackson would appear next. Continually caught off guard, they lost fight after fight. On June 8 and 9, Jackson took on two Union armies in two separate battles—and was victorious both days. It was a great morale booster for the South. Jackson himself was exultant. He told another general, "He who does not see the hand of God in this is blind, sir, blind!"

In October 1862, Jackson was promoted to lieutenant general and given control of the Second Corps of the Confederate army. "Old Blue Light"—as Jackson was also called because of his piercing blue eyes—was commander Robert E. Lee's most trusted colleague. He proved his military expertise again and again. At the Second Battle of Bull Run (also called Second Manassas), he held back the Union army until reinforcements could arrive—and then led the counterattack in person.

Stonewall seemed to be unbeatable. Crowds cheered him whenever he appeared in Richmond, the Confederate capital. Naturally, he was pleased to be regarded as a hero. But, as he reminded a friend, people shouldn't praise him. They should give "all to the glory of God."

Jackson's finest hour came at the Battle of Chancellorsville, in Virginia. At dusk on May 2, 1863, he led a secret attack on Union forces that made the Yankees run away in panic. His bold move achieved a surprise victory.

But the evening was not over yet. As the dark closed in, Jackson and some of his staff rode forward on a scouting mission. Some of their own troops mistook them for the enemy and started to shoot. Jackson was wounded once in his right hand and twice in his left arm. Because the bone was shattered, his arm had to be amputated.

The death of Stonewall ⚔ Jackson at the Chandler home outside Chancellorsville, on May 10, 1863.

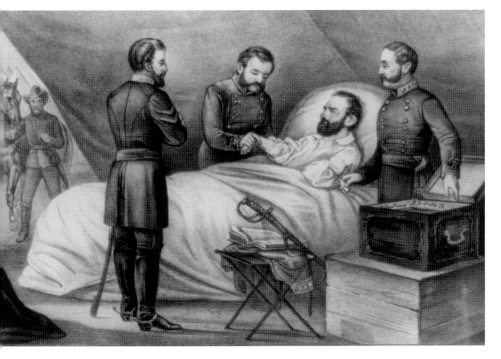

At first it looked as if Jackson would recover. But a few days later, pneumonia set in. On Sunday, May 10, Jackson was told he was going to die. "I have always desired to die on Sunday," he told his wife. A few hours later his delirium ceased and his face grew calm. Stonewall Jackson had finally found peace: "Let us cross over the river," he said, "and rest under the shade of the trees."

Oliver Wendell Holmes Jr. (1841–1935)

Young Yankee Soldier

Twenty years after he left the U.S. Army, Oliver Wendell Holmes Jr. wrote that his generation had been "set apart by its experience." "Through our great good fortune," he said, "in our youth our hearts were touched with fire. . . . We have seen with our own eyes . . . the snowy heights of honor." As an older man, Holmes could look back and see the war as a romantic adventure. It hadn't seemed so grand, though, when he was living through it.

The son of famous poet and essayist Oliver Wendell Holmes Sr., 21-year-old Holmes was just finishing up his degree at Harvard when the war began. He eventually obtained a commission as a lieutenant in the 20th Regiment of Massachusetts Volunteers and was sent down to Washington, D.C., where he trained with the Army of the Potomac. For the next three and a half years, Holmes fought in many major battles and was wounded three times.

His first taste of combat came at Ball's Bluff, Virginia, in October 1861, when his regiment was ambushed by the Confederates. Holmes himself was shot in the chest. "I felt as if a horse had kicked me," he wrote. Carried to a deserted house that had been turned into a temporary hospital, he was placed on the floor. He glanced across the room—and there, in a pool of blood, was a severed arm. He recognized it as that of a friend. "I closed my eyes with . . . sickening," he confided to his diary. Believing that he was going to die, Holmes made a doctor promise to tell his family he had done his duty. But the ball had managed to miss his heart and lungs and Holmes lived, recuperating at home in Massachusetts until March 1862. Then he rejoined the Army of the Potomac in the Virginia Peninsula, fighting illness, mosquitoes, and the enemy. He wrote to his parents, "As you go through the woods you stumble constantly, and if after dark . . . perhaps tread on the swollen bodies already fly blown and decaying, of men shot in the head, back, or bowels."

Holmes was wounded again at the Battle of Antietam on September 17, 1862, this time in the neck. The wound was plugged with lint and Holmes was sent home once more. Back at the front the next March, he felt the pessimism that had settled over the troops: "The army is tired with its hard and terrible experience. . . . I've pretty much made up my mind that the South have achieved their independence."

But that would not happen before Holmes was wounded for the last time, at Chancellorsville in May 1863. After this wound laid him up for

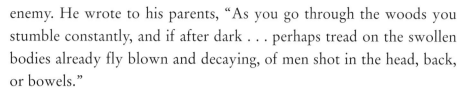

(below): Skulls of unburied soldiers killed at Chancellorsville.

(below, right): The Battle of Chancellorsville May 1–4, 1863. Holmes was one of the 30,000 casualties of the battle.

The justices of the Supreme Court in 1904. Justice Oliver Wendell Holmes Jr. is in the back row on the far left.

seven months, he returned, not as a soldier on the front lines but as an aide to General Horatio Wright. He was at the defense of Fort Stevens in Washington, D.C., when he spotted a tall civilian with a stovepipe hat on the lookout tower.

"Get down, you damned fool!" Holmes ordered as enemy bullets went whizzing by.

The tall man stepped down—and to his horror Holmes realized he had been talking to President Abraham Lincoln. "I'm glad you know how to talk to a civilian, Captain Holmes," the amused Lincoln told him later.

Holmes left the service soon afterward and went on to become a renowned judge, serving as justice of the Supreme Court for a record-breaking 30 years. After he died at age 94, two bloodstained uniforms and two musket balls were found in his closet, his mementos from a war fought 70 years before.

Sam Watkins (1839–1901)

Confederate "Webfoot"

"A private soldier is but an automaton [a robot]," Samuel Rush Watkins wrote. "His business is to load and shoot, stand picket, videt, etc., while the officers sleep, or perhaps die on the field of battle and glory. . . . He is soon forgotten."

Sam Watkins enlisted as a private in the First Tennessee Infantry, Company H, in the spring of 1861 and served for all four years of the war. Nearly 20 years later, he began to write a series of reminiscences for the Columbia *Herald*, which were then published as a book: *"Co. Aytch": A Side Show of the Big Show*. His ironic, modest, and moving memoirs have ensured that Sam Watkins, at least, is not forgotten.

The 21-year-old Watkins was attending Jackson College in Columbia, Tennessee, when the war started. After his enlistment he began fighting almost immediately and found himself in a long list of battles: Shiloh, Perryville, Murfreesboro, Chickamauga, and Atlanta,

(below): The battlefield at ⊠ Shiloh, April 1862, where Watkins fought. Shiloh was the bloodiest battle ever fought on American soil up until that time.

(below, right): Lee and ⊠ Gordon's Mill at Chickamauga, Georgia. The Battle of Chickamauga had the second-highest number of casualties in the war.

among others. After his first fight, he was amused to see that all the officers had torn the insignia of their rank off their uniforms. They thought the Yankees would "hunt for them and not hurt the privates," Sam said wryly. "I always shot at privates. It was they that did the shooting and killing, and if I could kill or wound a private, why, my chances were so much the better. I always looked upon officers as harmless personages."

Being in the army was one endless march for the "Webfoots," as Sam called the infantry. "Along the route it was nothing but tramp, tramp, tramp . . . through long and dusty lanes, weary, worn out, and hungry. . . . I have seen soldiers fast asleep and no doubt dreaming of home and loved ones there, as they staggered along in their places in the ranks. I know that on many a weary night's march I have slept, and slept soundly, while marching along in my proper place."

Foraging for food was a daily activity. One day, while marching along the Tennessee River, his company spied a cornfield across the river. The corn seemed to beckon to the weary soldiers: "Come hither, Johnny Reb." "The river was wide, but we were hungry," Watkins remembered. "We pulled off our clothes and launched into the turbid stream and were soon

⊠ (opposite, top): The battlefield at Kennesaw Mountain, Georgia, where Watkins's unit held the fort on June 27, 1864.

Union river transports on ⊠ Pittsburgh Landing on the Tennessee River, near Shiloh battlefield.

⊠ (opposite, bottom): The Confederate lines around Atlanta, where Sam Watkins participated in the battle of July 22, 1864.

on the other bank. Here was the field, and here were the roasting ears, but where was the raft or canoe?" Ever inventive, the rebels shucked the corn, tied the shucks together in a long train, and pulled the train of corn across the river with their mouths.

That was the lighter side of war. In battle after battle, Sam saw the horror as well. The view after the Battle of Chickamauga on September 19, 1863, was typically appalling: "The Confederate and Federal dead, wounded, and dying were everywhere scattered over the battlefield," he wrote. "You might . . . find men shot from the crown of the head to the tip end of the toe. And then to see all those dead, wounded, and dying horses. . . . "

✖ Sam Watkins's First Tennessee regiment helped lead the Confederates to victory at Chickamauga.

Peachtree Street in Atlanta ✉ after Federal bombardment of the city.

General Braxton Bragg, ✉ Sam Watkins's commanding officer in the Army of Tennessee at Shiloh and Chickamauga.

After four years of daily hardship and death, Watkins grew philosophical about the role of the common soldier: "Dying on the field of battle and glory is about the easiest duty a soldier has to undergo," he decided. "It is the living, marching, fighting, shooting soldier that has the hardships of war to carry. When a brave soldier is killed he is at rest. . . . The dead are heroes, the living are but men compelled to do the drudgery and suffer the privations incident to the thing called 'glorious war.'"

Of the 120 men who enlisted in Company H in the spring of 1861, only seven were still alive four years later. Sam Watkins was one of them.

William H. Carney (1840–1908)

Slave Turned Soldier

In January 1863, Governor Andrew of Massachusetts called for the first black regiment in the U.S. Army. Black leaders responded enthusiastically, understanding that black men finally had the chance to fight for the liberation of their race. "Men of Color, To Arms!" Frederick Douglass urged in his newspaper, *Douglass' Monthly*. The 1,000 men of the 54th Massachusetts, as the regiment was called, would aid in the acceptance of black soldiers throughout the North and help transform the Civil War into a war for black freedom. One of the men who enlisted in the winter of 1863 was a 22-year-old seaman from New Bedford, Massachusetts, named William Harvey Carney.

Born into slavery in Norfolk, Virginia, on February 29, 1840, Carney was lucky to be able to attend a secret school run by a local minister. His father, William, escaped from slavery in the late 1850s and went north to

✉ The guard house and guards of the 107th U.S. Colored Infantry.

New Bedford. Soon he had earned enough money to buy his family out of slavery, too. Carney was 23 when he enlisted in Company C of the 54th. In a letter to William Garrison's abolitionist newspaper, the *Liberator*, he explained why he enlisted: "Previous to the formation of colored troops, I had a strong inclination to prepare myself for the ministry; but when the country called for all persons, I could best serve my God [by] serving my country and my oppressed brothers."

Black troops knew they ran a special risk in battle. Although the rules of war stated that captured soldiers be exchanged or placed in prison camps, captured blacks were more likely to be killed on the spot or enslaved. The white officers who led the troops also knew that if they were captured, they could be executed. But one and all they were determined to show that black soldiers could fight as well and as bravely as white soldiers.

The troops' opportunity to prove themselves came on July 18, 1863, at Fort Wagner, fortifications outside Charleston Harbor. All day

Lincoln reading the first draft ⊠ of the Emancipation Proclamation to his cabinet, July 22, 1862. After the proclamation was issued in January 1863, black regiments started to be organized throughout the North.

Union warships bombarded the fort. When Federal commanders decided the Confederate threat had been reduced, they ordered an assault. The 54th Massachusetts, led by Colonel Robert Gould Shaw, was permitted to lead the charge. Carney recounted what happened next: "The regiment started to its feet, the charge being fairly commenced. We had got but a short distance when we were opened upon with musketry, shell, grape shot, and canister, which mowed down our men right and left. As the color-bearer became disabled, I threw away my gun and seized the colors [the American flag], making my way to the head of the column."

Carney carried the flag up to the fort itself and held on to it while the battle raged. Colonel Shaw himself was shot down when he leaped onto the wall. By the time the white regiments who were supposed to reinforce the 54th finally arrived, the battle had been lost. White and black soldiers alike started the dangerous retreat back across the sand. In the confusion, Carney thought he saw more Union troops ahead of him and raised his flag—only to discover they were rebels. Wheeling about, he crossed the moat and was hit by a bullet—and then another.

A soldier from the 100th New York saw that Carney was wounded and offered to carry the colors for him. Carney, though, would relinquish his burden to no one but a member of the 54th. Supported by the soldier, Carney staggered on and was wounded again, this time in the head. Finally, still holding the flag erect, he made it to the field hospital in the rear and found his regiment. "The men cheered me and the flag," Carney recalled. "My reply was, 'Boys, the old flag never touched the ground.'" Then he fainted.

In 1900, William Carney was awarded the Medal of Honor for his brave actions at Fort Wagner. The flag he carried is displayed in Memorial Hall, Boston.

Chapter Three

Civilian Heroes

Dorothea Dix (1802–1887)

Superintendent of Nurses

Dorothea Dix was a woman of action. So when Civil War hostilities began, she marched into the office of the acting surgeon of the Union army and told him the army needed her help. "I propose," she said, "to organize under the official auspices of the War Department, an Army Nursing Corps made up of women volunteers."

The 60-year-old reformer was accustomed to shaking things up. For the past 20 years, she had crusaded on behalf of the mentally ill: investigating the appalling care of the insane throughout the Northeast, petitioning state legislatures for reform, and founding hospitals. Now Dix proposed putting her boundless energy and ruthless efficiency to work on behalf of wounded soldiers. At first the Army medical corps was shocked by her proposal. An army hospital, with its suffering and blood and stench, was no place for a lady. But Dix was undeterred. She knew what miracles Florence Nightingale had wrought in the British army military hospitals during the Crimean War, and she was confident American women could do the same.

Eventually Dix wore the resistance down. In April 1861, she was appointed Superintendent of Women Nurses for the United States

Army. Dix interviewed every applicant for the military hospitals herself. She was looking for mature nurses who could withstand the stress of the hospital, "who can bear the presence of suffering and exercise entire self-control." Then, when she was overwhelmed by a flood of earnest young ladies, she issued a bulletin to the press: "No woman under 30 need apply to serve in government hospitals. All nurses are required to be plain looking women. Their dresses must be brown or black, with no bows, no curls, no jewelry, and no hoops." Dix wanted no romantic entanglements on her watch.

Stern and authoritarian, Dix was undoubtedly a difficult woman to work for. Some nurses called her "Dragon Dix" behind her back. But she was fiercely determined to improve care for the suffering soldiers. Medicine was still essentially medieval during the Civil War; the most common treatment for any kind of wound was amputation, since doctors took no antiseptic precautions to prevent infection and gangrene. But much could be done by nurses to provide comfort, increase cleanliness, and prolong life.

Dix worked without ceasing every day for four years, overseeing nurses, inspecting hospitals, and reporting abuse and mismanagement wherever she found it. Female nurses under her supervision received $12 per month (male nurses were paid $20.50 per month). Dix herself received nothing. When the war was over, Secretary of War Edwin Stanton asked Dix how she would like her services recognized. She asked merely for an American flag. It came, with the following tribute: "In acknowledgement of the inestimable services rendered by Miss Dorothea L. Dix for the care, succor, and relief of the sick and wounded soldiers of the United States on the battlefield, in the camps, and hospitals during the recent war."

⊠ Dorothea Dix in about 1850. She liked the photograph, remarking that it was "the only picture that seems to me a good likeness, and to convey something of the *tone* and *type* of character."

⊠ The Bloomingdale Asylum in New York City in the 19th century. In her lifetime, Dix founded or improved 32 hospitals for the mentally ill.

Mathew Brady (1822–1896)

Photographer of History

The haunting faces of Civil War soldiers look out at us from a thousand photographs—still, solemn, determined. Although there were as many as 200 photographers in the field during the war, the name that most of us know is Mathew Brady's. It was his vision that gave us the extraordinary historical record we have today.

Photography was in its infancy when young Brady studied the new art of daguerreotyping with Samuel F. B. Morse in the early 1840s. Brady opened his own first gallery at 205 Broadway in New York City in 1844. Although his failing eyesight soon forced him to delegate the actual camera work to his assistants, the artistic vision

(below): Mathew Brady in ⊠ 1875. Because of Brady's artistic vision and entrepreneurial energy, we have an unparalleled photographic record of the Civil War.

(below, right): A "what's it" ⊠ wagon—a mobile photographic darkroom—at Petersburg in 1864.

of Brady's studio remained his alone. Determined to record history, Brady took a photograph of every American president but one, from John Quincy Adams to William McKinley. He pursued all the great men of the time, begging them to pose for him. One day in 1860, the young Edward, Prince of Wales, walked into Brady's studio and had a photo taken of his whole entourage.

The most influential photograph of Brady's career, shot on February 27, 1860, was of a homely, nearly unknown Illinois politician named Abraham Lincoln. Lincoln asked to have his portrait taken while he was visiting New York to give a speech at Cooper Union. The speech was an overwhelming success and so was the photograph, which was sent to newspapers and magazines throughout the land. "Brady and the Cooper Union speech made me president," Lincoln said when he welcomed Brady to the White House the next year.

His friendship with Lincoln came in handy when war began and Brady decided it was his mission to photograph it. Although some pictures had been taken of the Mexican War in 1848 and England's Crimean War in 1855, no complete photographic record of a war had ever been attempted. When Brady asked Lincoln for permission to follow the Union army, Lincoln gave him a card on which he wrote "Pass Brady. A. Lincoln."

In July 1861, Brady heard there was going to be a great battle at Bull Run in Northern Virginia. "Destiny overruled me," he wrote later. "I felt I had to go, a spirit in my feet said, 'go,' and I went." He outfitted himself with a portable darkroom and wore a long linen duster and broad-brimmed hat. When Union soldiers were routed and panicked mobs rushed past him, his wagon was overturned. It took Brady three days to get back to Washington, carrying whatever glass plates he could salvage. When he arrived he had a photograph of himself taken. It was inscribed with the proud words "Brady the Photographer returned from Bull Run."

Eventually Brady had as many as 20 teams of men assigned to all parts of the army. Soldiers grew used to the photographers' "what's it?" wagons ("What's it?" is what soldiers would ask the first time they saw one) in the army camps. They would line up to have their photographs taken, sometimes small pictures known as "cartes de visite" that could be sent to loved ones back home. Because all subjects had to be posed for several seconds, action shots of the actual battles were impossible. For this reason, photographs of the Civil War seem stiff and posed: a general and his staff, supplies piled up at a railway depot, crewmembers cooking on an ironclad ship. No one ever seemed to smile.

The dead at Dunker Church after the Battle of Antietam, September 1862, one of Brady's 70 Civil War images.

The stillest shots of all are photographs of the dead. When Brady's pictures of the Battle of Antietam were displayed in New York in 1862, a *New York Times* writer wrote: "Mr. Brady has done something to bring home to us the terrible reality and earnestness of war. If he has not brought bodies and laid them in our dooryards and along the streets, he has done something very like it." After Brady, it became impossible to ignore the devastation that war could bring.

His historical project cost Brady more than $100,000, and he never made his money back. After the war, people wanted to forget the trauma the nation had suffered, and Brady had a hard time selling his photographs. Only now, many years later, do we recognize his priceless photographic record as the nation's treasured legacy.

⊠ Robert Smalls after the war. The slave turned Civil War hero became a U.S. Congressman from South Carolina during Reconstruction.

Robert Smalls (1839–1915)

Daring Steamship Pilot

On May 13, 1862, the commander of the USS *Onward*, a sailing ship posted outside Charleston Harbor, spotted an armed Confederate steamer heading his way. He was about to give the order to fire when a white flag was hoisted up the steamer's mast. The steamer was being surrendered to the Union army—and it was piloted by an enslaved African American. Robert Smalls had escaped from slavery by stealing a Confederate ship!

The man who had accomplished this breathtaking feat was born into slavery on April 5, 1839, in Beaufort, South Carolina. When he was a teenager, his master had hired him out for wages, and Robert eventually became a skilled boatman on the Charleston waterfront. Because he was only five feet five inches (165 cm) tall, he was often called "Small Robert." Born with no last name, Robert decided to adopt "Smalls" as his.

A cartoon honoring the career of Robert Smalls.

In 1861, the steamer Smalls was working on, the 150-foot (46 m) *Planter*, was turned into a Confederate army ferry and supply boat. The Confederates still held Fort Sumter at the head of Charleston Harbor. But out beyond the harbor was a blockading fleet of Union ships. Smalls knew that if he could just make it out as far as the blockade, he, his wife, and his child would be free.

He discussed his plans with the other nine slaves aboard the *Planter*. Then, in the early morning hours of May 13, 1862, when the white officers had gone ashore for the night, Smalls fired up the ship's boilers and ran the Confederate flag up the mast. First he picked up his family and the families of the other crewmen from a nearby steamer, where they had been hiding. The *Planter* headed out of the harbor. When they passed Fort Johnson, Smalls gave the usual whistle signal. The sentry let him pass. Then Smalls put on the captain's gold-trimmed coat and straw hat. As the *Planter* steamed past Fort Sumter, Smalls gave the whistle cord two long pulls and one short pull. Again, the sentry let him pass.

Now he only had to make it out past the range of Fort Sumter's guns. Smalls put on the steam and headed out the three miles (5 km) to the blockade. He was free.

Recognizing Smalls's invaluable knowledge of South Carolina waterways, the Union navy put him to use as a pilot. Captain Samuel Du Pont, commander of the blockading squadron, wrote to Secretary of the Navy Gideon Welles: "This man, Robert Smalls, is superior to any who has yet come into our lines, intelligent as many of them have been. . . . I shall continue to employ Robert as a pilot on board the *Planter* for inland waters."

President Lincoln signed a bill that actually awarded Smalls and the other crewmen $4,584, half the value of the *Planter* and her cargo; Smalls himself was awarded $1,500 of this sum. With this money Smalls was able to establish a home for his family in his birthplace of Beaufort, now controlled by Union soldiers. He had a very busy war, piloting the *Planter* and other Union vessels between various Federal posts along the coast. At the end of the war, he attended the flag-raising ceremony at Fort Sumter.

Smalls lived a long and distinguished life, serving in the South Carolina legislature and also in the U.S. House of Representatives from 1875 to 1879 and from 1881 to 1887. In 1889, he was appointed collector of the port of Beaufort.

Rose O'Neal Greenhow (1815–1864)

Spy in Petticoats

Beautiful, charming, and quick-witted, Rose O'Neal Greenhow was the perfect Washington society hostess. She was also the perfect Confederate spy.

Born on a Maryland plantation, Rose O'Neal came to Washington, D.C., at age 16 to live with her aunt. After she married, the Greenhow home became known as the place to see and be seen. When her husband died, Rose continued to entertain.

Rose O'Neal Greenhow with her eight-year-old daughter, Little Rose, at the Old Capitol prison in Washington, D.C., in spring 1862.

By the time the Civil War began, Greenhow had many influential friends. She made no secret of her sympathies with the South, yet continued to live in the Union capital. To Northerners, she said it was because Washington was her home. But secretly it was because she wanted to serve her "nation"—the Confederacy—as a spy.

In spring 1861, Greenhow was visited by Thomas Jordan, a captain in the U.S. Army who would shortly resign to join the Confederate military. He proposed that she become the Washington director of Southern espionage. Greenhow agreed enthusiastically. Soon she had a network of informants in military offices, on ships, and in the offices of undersecretaries and congressmen.

In early July, she discovered that Union general Irvin McDowell and his army of 30,000 had plans to march on the Confederate troops stationed at Manassas Junction, in northern Virginia. She sent two messages relaying the Union plans, specifying the number of men in the Union march and when they would be coming.

Greenhow's messages gave Confederate general Pierre G. T. Beauregard the information he needed to prepare for Union attack. On July 21, the rebels beat back the Federal forces in the first battle of the Civil War, at Manassas (called Bull Run by the Union). Greenhow was jubilant.

⊠ A view of the First Battle of Bull Run, July 21, 1861. It was the first real battle of the Civil War.

Confederate general Pierre G.
T. Beauregard won a victory at
First Bull Run, aided by the
intelligence reports of Rose
O'Neal Greenhow.

But the well-known hostess was being watched. A month later, after suspicious papers were found in her home, she was arrested by Union detective Allan Pinkerton. At first she was imprisoned in her own home, along with other women suspected of being agents. Then she and her eight-year-old daughter were transferred to the Old Capitol prison. In March 1862, she was tried by the War Department. Greenhow denied everything, adding, however, that she would certainly have passed information on to the Confederates if she had had it. "I am a Southern woman," she said proudly, "and I thank God that no drop of Yankee blood ever polluted my veins." The commission sentenced Rose Greenhow to exile in the Confederacy.

"But for you there would have been no Battle of Bull Run," Confederate president Jefferson Davis said when he greeted Rose. He had another job for her to do: plead the Confederate cause overseas, in England and France. In August 1863, Greenhow traveled to Europe aboard a blockade runner. Armed with letters from Davis, she met with British and French officials. She also published a book, *My Imprisonment and the First Year of Abolition Rule in Washington.*

Her mission accomplished, Greenhow set off for home in August 1864, again on a blockade runner. When her ship was run aground after being spied by a Union gunboat, she tried to escape in a small rowboat. It capsized, and Greenhow drowned. It was said that she was dragged underwater by the weight of the gold coins she had sewn into her skirts—gold that she was bringing back to her beloved Confederacy.

Rose O'Neal Greenhow was buried with full military honors in Wilmington, South Carolina.

Charlotte Forten (1837–1914)

Teacher and Activist

In the midst of the Civil War, a young black woman named Charlotte Forten traveled to the Sea Islands off the coast of South Carolina to teach the children of ex-slaves. It was a brave act, since any black person who traveled south ran the risk of capture and being sold into slavery. Yet Charlotte was used to acting on her principles. She was the granddaughter of James Forten, a Philadelphia merchant who fought in the Revolutionary War and was one of the nation's first black abolitionists. Courage ran in her family.

⊠ Charlotte Forten was the first Northern African-American schoolteacher to go south to teach former slaves.

Charlotte Forten grew up in Philadelphia in comfortable circumstances, in a close circle of free black people and abolitionists. Because of pervasive racial prejudice, she was educated at home. At age 16, she left for Salem, Massachusetts, where she studied to be a teacher. There, in 1854, she wrote the first entry in a journal that she kept on and off for the next 30 years and that was destined to make her famous: "I wish to record the passing events of my life, which even if quite unimportant to others, naturally possess great interest to myself." A sensitive and intelligent young woman, she agonized over the position of black people in her country. "Oh, that I could do much toward bettering our condition. I will do *all*, all the *very little* that lies in my power, while life and strength last."

When the Civil War started, she had her chance. In October 1862, Forten arrived in Port Royal, South Carolina, "in the very heart of

Rebeldom," to teach at a school for free slaves. Although South Carolina was still Confederate, Union soldiers had landed on the Sea Islands on November 7, 1861. Charlotte would never forget her first meeting with her students: "I noticed with pleasure how bright, how eager to learn many of them seem. . . . Dear children, born in slavery but free at last! . . . My heart goes out to you. I shall be glad to do all that I can to help you."

During the day, Forten and the other teachers taught the children to read and write; in the evening, they taught the adults. She in turn learned much from the former slaves: their stories of tribulation, their African traditions, and the dances and "shouts" they kept alive on the Islands.

The following summer, the 54th Massachusetts, the first black regiment organized after the Emancipation Proclamation, came to Port Royal. Forten had a chance to become friends with Colonel Robert Gould Shaw, the young white commander of the regiment. In a letter to his parents, Shaw described the impressive young woman of 25: "She is quite pretty, remarkably well educated, and a very interesting woman. She is decidedly the belle here, and the officers of both the army and the navy seem to think her society far preferable to that of the other ladies."

Shaw was destined to die less than a month later in a heroic assault on Fort Wagner, outside Charleston. When she first heard the dreadful news, Forten volunteered as a nurse to help tend the wounded soldiers of the 54th. "Brave fellows," she wrote in her diary. "I feel it a happiness, an honor, to do the slightest service for them. . . . it is the testimony of all that they fought bravely as men can fight."

Forten taught at Port Royal on and off until the end of the war and later in freedman's schools. She remained active and interested in black rights until the day she died. As her husband, the Reverend Francis Grimke, said of her, "She never grew old in spirit."

Walt Whitman (1819–1892)

Civil War Poet

⊠ Walt Whitman

In 1860, a newspaperman named Walt Whitman saw Abraham Lincoln visit New York City on his inaugural tour. He noticed "his perfect composure and coolness—his unusual and uncouth height, his dress of complete black, stovepipe hat push'd back on the head." An extraordinary, self-taught poet, Whitman would see Lincoln many more times in the next four years. And, as it happened, he would write his best-known epitaph.

Born in Huntington, New York, to a farming family, Whitman had many jobs—errand boy, teacher, journalist, typesetter, carpenter—before he published the first edition of his controversial book of poems, *Leaves of Grass*, in 1855. Some people, the famous author Ralph Waldo Emerson among them, praised the volume for its original American voice. Many more were outraged by its unconventional verse and subject matter. Undeterred, Whitman would revise and add to the slender volume for the rest of his life.

Whitman was in New York in 1861 when he first heard the news that the Civil War had begun. Like many people, his first reaction was militant and intensely patriotic:

Beat! beat! drums!—blow! bugles! blow!
Through the windows—through doors—burst like a ruthless force,
Into the solemn church, and scatter the congregation,
Into the school where the scholar is studying;
So fierce you whirr and pound you drums—so shrill you bugles blow.

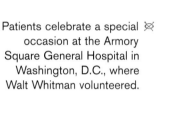

Patients celebrate a special occasion at the Armory Square General Hospital in Washington, D.C., where Walt Whitman volunteered.

As the war went on and casualty lists were published, Whitman's enthusiasm waned. He started visiting Manhattan hospitals and nursing wounded soldiers. When his brother George was listed as wounded after the Battle of Fredericksburg in December 1862, Whitman left to find him in Washington, D.C. What he saw on the battlefield and in the hospitals changed his view of the war forever. "Now that I have lived for eight or nine days amid such scenes as the camps furnish," Whitman wrote to his mother back in Brooklyn, "really nothing we call trouble seems worth talking about." He decided to serve as a volunteer in the military hospitals.

Whitman's role was to clean and bandage wounds, to visit the men and write letters for them, and to assist with amputations. His poem

"The Wound-Dresser" describes in graphic detail the suffering that he witnessed:

> *On, on I go (open doors of time! open hospital*
> *   doors!)*
> *The crush'd head I dress (poor crazed hand tear*
> *   not the bandages away),*
> *The neck of the cavalry-man with the bullet*
> *   through and through I examine,*
> *Hard the breathing rattles, quite glazed already*
> *   the eye, yet life struggles hard,*
> *(Come, sweet death! be persuaded O beautiful*
> *   death! In mercy come quickly).*

Whitman turned against the war. "My opinion is to stop the war now," he said. He was back in Brooklyn with his mother in April 1865 when he heard that the war was finally over—and, a week later, that Lincoln had been assassinated. As before, Whitman chose to express his intense feelings in poetry. In "O Captain! My Captain!" he compares Lincoln to the captain of a ship that has successfully completed a long voyage. "The fearful trip is done," the speaker says. But then the unthinkable happens:

> *But O heart! heart! heart!*
> * O the bleeding drops of red,*
> *   Where on the deck my Captain lies,*
> *   Fallen cold and dead.*

Written in conventional rhyme and meter, "O Captain! My Captain!" earned great public acclaim. Whitman's greatest poem of mourning, though, is "When Lilacs Last in the Dooryard Bloom'd," a more subtle, difficult, and lyrical tribute to Lincoln. In it, he comes to terms with the death of Lincoln and those fallen in battle:

I saw battle-corpses, myriads of them,
And the white skeletons of young men, I saw them,
I saw the débris and débris of all the slain soldiers of the war. . . .

After the war ended, the nation was reborn and like the lilac, "blooming, returning with spring." And of the fallen soldiers Whitman said:

. . . and their memory ever to keep, for the dead I loved so well,
For the sweetest, wisest soul of all my days and lands—and this
        for his dear sake,
Lilac and star and bird twined with the chant of my soul,
There in the fragrant pines and the cedars dusk and dim.

Walt Whitman always looked on his calling as "Soldier's Missionary" as the most fulfilling role of his life. And because he was also a great poet—some say America's greatest—he was able to transform four years of tumult and tragedy into lasting works of art.

Further Reading

Beller, Susan P. *To Hold This Ground: A Desperate Battle at Gettysburg.* New York: Simon & Schuster, 1995.

Clinton, Catherine. *Scholastic Encyclopedia of the Civil War.* New York: Scholastic, 1999.

Cox, Clinton. *Undying Glory: The Story of the Massachusetts 54th Regiment.* New York: Scholastic, 1991.

Hakim, Joy. *War, Terrible War: A History of Us.* New York: Oxford University Press, 1994.

Hoobler, Dorothy, and Thomas Hoobler. *Photographing History: The Career of Mathew Brady.* New York: G. P. Putnam's Sons, 1977.

Katcher, Philip. *The Civil War Source Book.* New York: Facts on File, 1992.

McPherson, James M. *Fields of Fury: The Civil War.* New York: Atheneum, 2002.

Nolan, Jeannette Covert. *Spy for the Confederacy: Rose O'Neal Greenhow.* New York: Julian Messner, Inc., 1962.

Reef, Catherine. *Walt Whitman.* New York: Clarion Books, 1995.

Schleichert, Elizabeth. *The Life of Dorothea Dix.* Frederick, Md.: Twenty-First Century Books, 1992.

Shaara, Michael. *The Killer Angels.* New York: David McKay Co., 1974. Reprint, New York: Ballantine, 1975.

White, G. Edward. *Oliver Wendell Holmes: Sage of the Supreme Court.* New York: Oxford University Press, 2000.

Zeinert, Karen. *Those Courageous Women of the Civil War.* Brookfield, Conn.: The Millbrook Press, 1998.

Glossary

Abolition—The act of abolishing, or getting rid of, slavery.

Blockade—The blocking of an enemy shore or harbor by warships or troops.

Brigade—A large body of troops made up of two or more regiments and commanded by a brigadier general.

Casualty—A soldier who is killed, wounded, or missing.

Cavalry—The branch of an army that is mounted on horseback.

Confederate—A person who was a citizen of the Confederate States of America.

Confederate States of America—The name of the nation formed by the 11 states that seceded from the United States in 1860 and 1861.

Constitutional Convention (1787)—The meeting of delegates in Philadelphia who wrote a constitution for the United States.

Corps—A tactical unit of the army made up of two or more divisions.

Crimean War (1854-56)—A war fought by Great Britain, France, and Turkey against Russia for control of the Black Sea and the eastern Mediterranean.

Freedman's Bureau—The government agency established to help former slaves.

Gettysburg Address (1863)—The speech given by President Lincoln after the Battle of Gettysburg.

Infantry—The branch of an army composed of soldiers who fight on foot.

Medal of Honor—The highest military award in the United States.

Mexican War (1846-48)—War fought against Mexico that gave the United States California and New Mexico.

Minié Ball—A rifle bullet with a soft, cone-shaped head.

Musket—A shoulder gun carried by the infantry.

Regiment—A military unit of about 350 troops, usually commanded by a colonel.

Revolutionary War (1776-83)—The war fought by the 13 states against Great Britain for American independence.

Secede—To withdraw from or leave an organization.

Secessionist—In the Civil War, someone who believed in the right of a state to separate from the United States.

Shenandoah Valley Campaign—Confederate general Stonewall Jackson's campaign in Virginia's Shenandoah Valley.

Slavery—The state of one person being owned by another.

Union—During the Civil War, the states that did not secede from the United States of America.

West Point—The academy that prepares officers for the United States Army.

Index